Abraham H. Maslow

Abraham H. Maslow

Maslow

His Theory of Human Nature
and Its Social Implications

RUSSAEL JOANNES

ISBN: 979-8-9887087-7-3 (Hardback)
ISBN: 979-8-9887087-0-4 (Paperback)
ISBN: 979-8-9887087-1-1 (Ebook)

Library of Congress Control Number: 2023912658

Front cover image by Artist: *the*BookDesigners.com
Book design by Designer: *the*BookDesigners.com

First printing edition 2023

Published by
Russael Joannes
www.russael.com

Dedication

For Abraham Maslow

Table of Contents

Maslow and I

I FIRST CAME ACROSS the work of Abraham Maslow in the used section of Kepler's Books in Menlo Park, California. The book was *The Farther Reaches of Human Nature*. I went on to read his *Motivation and Personality* and *Eupsychian Management*. I was thirty years old, in graduate school. In my whole life up to that time there had been no mention about the heights a human might aspire to, other than what I'd picked up in history and novels.

I went on to read other psychologists and psychoanalysts: Jung, Rogers, Erikson. I tried Freud. Erikson's works on identity gripped me; I read his *Young Man Luther* and *Gandhi's Truth*. At one point I read Jung's *Symbols of Transformation* by day and dreamt a whole dream cycle by night.

My interest now lies with political theory. As part of that endeavor, one starts with human nature. This led me back to Maslow. Rereading Maslow, I was surprised anew at the beauty of his prose and vision. Maslow was one of many humanistic psychologists, but he was the greatest synthesizer and theorist among them, providing some system to their collective discoveries. At the same time his writings explode in many directions, as he teases out the implications of his theories.

Preface

THIS BOOK IS A SYNOPSIS of the six main books of Abraham Maslow, not a biography.

What the biographies provide is the record of his life and his growth as a psychologist. You may find a couple of scholarly biographies of Maslow in *Further Reading*. There are also histories of the humanistic psychology movement.

My intent in this book is different. It is to say succinctly what Maslow says in his published books. These books represent his mature thinking, and they subsume or gather his most important papers. My method in this book is to provide brief explanations of his thought followed by direct quotes.

I include topics often slighted by other writers on Maslow. Most of them focus on Maslow's psychology, which, of course, is the crux of his theory.

But Maslow was also a societal thinker. He analyzed education, the workplace, science, and religion in the light of his theories. Had he lived longer, he would have published a book on politics. These social psychologies have not received nearly the attention that his psychology has received. They are more fully addressed in this work.

There is no substitute for reading Maslow himself. The current book, however, will put you on the gameboard, and you can find your way from there.

BIOGRAPHICAL SKETCH OF ABRAHAM MASLOW

Abraham Maslow was born in 1908 of Russian Jewish immigrants in Brooklyn, New York. He began his professional work with the behavioral study of monkey sexuality and dominance. Later, he discovered psychoanalysis, anthropology, gestalt, and related theories, and switched his work to the study of human beings in the clinic, resulting in the work which is the content of this book. Maslow died in in Menlo Park, California 1970.

HUMANISTIC PSYCHOLOGY

Humanistic psychology was a reaction in the middle years of the twentieth century to behaviorism and to the Freudian focus on psychopathology. It was therefore sometimes referred to as the Third Force in psychology. Humanistic psychology considered that there was a healthy side to human beings, a striving toward full humanness, even spirituality.

ABBREVIATIONS

B-values • Being-values
SA • Self-actualization
In citations:
Being • The Psychology of Being
EM • Eupsychian Management
FR • The Farther Reaches of Human Nature
M&P • Motivation and Personality
Religion • Religion, Values, and Peak Experiences
Science • The Psychology of Science

SCOPE

The books synopsized here are his six published books:

Motivation and Personality, 1954, revised 1970. In this book you will find the classic description of the hierarchy of needs and of self-actualization. The preface of the second edition alone is a golden overview of his work.

Toward a Psychology of Being, 1962. A continuation of Motivation and Personality.

The Farther Reaches of Human Nature, 1971. A wide-ranging collection of papers on various topics, such as education, transcendence, values, synergy, Synanon, and Theory Y.

Eupsychian Management, 1965. A journal Maslow kept while on sabbatical at Non-Linear Systems, Inc., Del Mar, California. The book was reissued as *Maslow on Management*, 1998, with two short essays on existentialism omitted, various anecdotes by others added, and minor vocabulary changes.

Religion, Values, and Peak-Experiences, 1964, 1970. A short book whose title describes its content.

The Psychology of Science: A Reconnaissance, 1966. A short, dense book examining the need for values and love in science.

ONE

Maslow's Theory of Human Nature

I. Introduction

AT THE CORE OF ABRAHAM MASLOW'S WORK is the vision that human beings have a higher nature, and that the striving to realize this higher nature is the defining feature of human life.

To realize this higher nature each human being must fulfill their *basic needs*, from physiological to esteem. Once these are satisfied, the human is motivated by the highest need, that is, for self-actualization.

Because these needs are seen as valuable by human beings, they provide an *innate value system* for humankind. The culmination of this value system is what Maslow calls the *Being-values*, or *B-values*, including such values as truth, justice, beauty, and goodness.

Along the way to higher psychological health most people have *peak experiences*, that is, mystical moments of ecstasy, which can propel them on their way to full humanness.

These four parts combine to make up Maslow's theory of human nature: human needs, self-actualization, peak experiences, and human values.

II. Human Needs

ONE OF THE GREAT FORERUNNERS of humanistic psychology was psychoanalysis. Freud and others had amassed out of their analysis sessions a "huge, rich, and illuminating literature of dynamic psychology and psychopathology, a great store of information on man's weaknesses and fears. We know much about why men do wrong things, why they bring about their own unhappiness and their self-destruction, why they are perverted and sick." (Being, 139)

This body of knowledge remained essential to Maslow, even as he focused on the higher aspects of human nature. For while many humans are striving to grow, many are still unhealthy, and even among the healthiest human beings, none are perfect:

> Human life will never be understood unless its highest aspirations are taken into account ... And yet there are also other regressive, fearful, self-diminishing tendencies as well, and it is very easy to forget them in our intoxication with "personal growth".... I consider that a necessary prophylactic against such illusions is a thorough knowledge of psychopathology and of depth psychology. ... Freud is still required reading for the humanistic psychologist (his facts, not his metaphysics). (M&P, xii-xiii)

Thus, psychopathologies were not evidence that human beings were bad, however, they were evidence of the thwarting of their higher nature:

Freud, Adler, Jung, and the rest agreed in this, that in their efforts to understand the origins of adult neurosis, they all wound up with biologically demanding needs violated or neglected early in life. Neurosis seemed to be in its essence a deficiency disease of the same sort that the nutritionists were discovering. (Science, 68)

HUMANITY'S HIGHER NATURE

Maslow and the other humanistic psychologists set out to amend Freud by adding the higher side of human nature:

"To oversimplify the matter somewhat, it is as if Freud supplied to us the sick half of psychology and we must now fill it out with the healthy half." (Being, 15)

"Growth, self-actualization, the striving toward health, the quest for identity and autonomy, the yearning for excellence ... must by now be accepted beyond question as a widespread and perhaps universal human tendency." (M&P, xii-xiii)

MASLOW'S HIERARCHY OF NEEDS

To achieve psychological health, the human being must gratify a hierarchy of needs. "[T]he human being has ... not only physiological needs, but also truly psychological ones. They may be considered as deficiencies which must be optimally fulfilled by the environment in order to avoid sickness and subjective ill-being." (Being, 129)

"The easiest technique for releasing the organism from the bondage of the lower, more material, more selfish needs is to gratify them." (M&P, 61)

The needs must be met in order from lowest to highest.

1. Physiological, i.e., hunger. Physiological needs must be met first. "For our chronically and extremely hungry man, Utopia can be defined simply as a place where there is plenty of food." (M&P, 37)

2. Safety. "[S]ecurity; stability; dependency; protection; freedom from fear, from anxiety and chaos; need for structure, order, law, limits; strength in the protector; and so on". (M&P, 39)

3. Love and Belonging. Frustration of the love need is a primary source of neuroses; gratification of the love need is the one sure foundation for higher psychological health. "It is agreed by practically all therapists that when we trace a neurosis back to its beginnings we shall find with great frequency a deprivation of love in the early years." (M&P, 275)

4. Esteem. "All people in our society (with a few pathological exceptions) have a need or desire for a stable, firmly based, usually high evaluation of themselves, for self-respect, or self-esteem, and for the esteem of others." (M&P, 45)

5. Self-actualization. To become what one is. See *Self-actualization* below.

Maslow also postulates two additional needs—for knowledge and beauty:

"The needs for knowledge, for understanding, for a life philosophy, for a theoretical frame of reference, for a value system, these are themselves ... a part of our primitive and animal nature (we are very special animals)." (M&P, 101)

"[I]n some individuals there is a truly basic aesthetic need. They get sick (in special ways) from ugliness, and are cured by beautiful surroundings; they crave actively, and their cravings can be satisfied only by beauty. It is seen universally in healthy children." (M&P, 51)

As each need is gratified, it drops out of consciousness, and the next higher need emerges. Humans focus on the tier of need they are on and may not even be aware of lower and higher needs. The lower needs have dropped out of awareness because satisfied; the higher needs have not yet emerged into awareness.

> [I]t looks as if there were a single ultimate value for mankind, a far goal toward which all men strive… But it is also true that the person himself does not know this… So far as he is concerned, the absolute, ultimate value, synonymous with life itself, is whichever need in the hierarchy he is dominated by during a particular period. (Being, 130-131)

Of course, life is messier than a single hierarchy or ladder, to be climbed rung by rung. There is overlap between the levels of need, and some individuals may seek to gratify a "higher need" prior to a "lower." That is, for a given individual, the order of need gratification may vary. "In actual fact, most members of our society who are normal are partially satisfied in all their basic needs and partially unsatisfied in all their basic needs at the same time." (M&P, 53-54)

III. Self-actualization

AT THE PINNACLE of the hierarchy of needs is the need for self-actualization. This is the need to know one's identity and to achieve full humanness.

Self-actualization is different from the lower needs in that it can begin to be addressed early in life, even before the basic needs are gratified. It starts with the search for identity, strengths, talents, and tastes. These are not arbitrary but instead emerge from the innermost being of the person. Once the lower needs are gratified, the need to self-actualize becomes the main motivation of the person.

GENESIS OF SELF-ACTUALIZATION

To begin with, Maslow drew his evidence of self-actualization from teachers he revered. He was particularly adoring of anthropologist Ruth Benedict and psychologist Max Wertheimer. He said of them: "It was as if they were not quite people... but something more than people." They were "very, very wonderful people."

He wanted to understand "why these two people were so different from the run-of-the-mill people in the world." He took copious notes on their personality characteristics. Then in "one wondrous moment," he realized that their pattern of personality could be generalized, suggesting that he had discovered a new kind of human being. (FR, 41-42)

Maslow adopted the term self-actualization from the German psychologist Kurt Goldstein. In treating WWI brain-injured soldiers Goldstein discovered that despite their injuries they seemed to have a resilience and an intrinsic striving toward wholeness. (Being, 27)

Maslow found corroboration of self-actualization in the work of many other thinkers. "Among psychiatrists, psychoanalysts, and psychologists it has been found necessary by Goldstein, Bühler, Jung, Horney, Fromm, Rogers, and many others." (M&P, 78) Maslow also "tapped the immense literatures of mysticism, religion, art, creativeness, love, etc." (Being, 66)

THE WORK OF A LIFETIME

Self-actualization is the work of a lifetime. It amounts to a transcendence of life, having experienced it all. One of the best descriptions of self-actualization is Maslow's description of why it takes so long:

> By the criteria I used, self-actualization does not occur in young people. In our culture at least, youngsters have not yet achieved identity, or autonomy, nor have they had time enough to experience an enduring, loyal, post-romantic love relationship, nor have they generally found their calling, the altar upon which to offer themselves. Nor have they worked out their own system of values; nor have they had experience enough (responsibility for others, tragedy, failure, achievement, success) to shed perfectionistic illusions and become realistic; nor have they generally made their peace with death; nor have they learned how to be patient; nor have they learned enough about evil in themselves and others to be compassionate; nor have they had time to become post-ambivalent about parents and elders, power and authority; nor have they generally become knowledgeable and educated enough to open the possibility of becoming wise; nor have

they generally acquired enough courage to be unpopular, to be unashamed about being openly virtuous, etc. (M&P, xx)

That is, self-actualization requires "working through":

Instant self-actualization, in a great moment of conversion or insight or awakening does happen, but it is extremely rare and should not be counted upon. The psychoanalysts ... now stress "working through", the long, slow, painful, repeated effort to use and to apply the insights. In the East, spiritual teachers and guides will generally also make this same point, that to improve oneself is a lifelong effort. (M&P, 257-258)

QUALITIES OF SELF-ACTUALIZING PERSONS

Maslow delineates a number of qualities of the self-actualizing person. Among these are the following:

DEVOTED WORK

Self-actualizing persons each have a task in the world that they have devoted themselves to.

These individuals customarily have some mission in life, some task to fulfill, some problem outside themselves which enlists much of their energies. This is not necessarily a task that they would prefer or choose for themselves; it may be a task that they feel is their responsibility, duty, or obligation. (M&P, 159)

PROFOUND LOVE

Self-actualizing persons love deeply and are deeply loved. "Self-actualizing people have deeper and more profound interpersonal relations than any other adults… They are capable of more fusion, greater love, more perfect identification, more obliteration of the ego boundaries than other people would consider possible." (M&P, 166)

CLARITY OF PERCEPTION

Self-actualizing persons perceive more clearly because their needs have been gratified. Their perception is not clouded by needing something from the other. "Fully disinterested, desireless, objective and holistic perception of another human being becomes possible only when nothing is needed from him, only when he is not needed." (Being, 38)

Self-actualizers see so clearly that they can be likened to the child in Hans Christian Andersen's *The Emperor's New Clothes* who among all the spectators sees that the king has no clothes. (Being, 118)

CLARITY OF LOVING PERCEPTION

Love allows the lover to see the beloved more clearly.

"[F]ar from accepting the common platitude that love makes people blind, I become more and more inclined to think of the *opposite* as true, namely that non-love makes us blind." (Being, 44)

Love allows the lover to see the true virtues of the beloved.

[I]t cannot be emphasized strongly enough that this miraculous capacity which love bestows on the lovers consists in the power to discover in the object of love virtues which it actually possesses but which are invisible to the uninspired; they are not invented by the lover, who decorates the beloved with illusory values: love is no self-deception... No doubt there is a strong emotional element in it but essentially love is a cognitive act indeed the only way to grasp the innermost core of personality. (Oswald Schwarz, quoted in M&P, 200)

The most profound love is that of self-actualizing persons. Maslow coined the term *B-love*, or *Being-love*, to characterize this level of love.

"The truest, most penetrating perception of the other is made possible by B-love. (Being, 44)

This does not mean that the lover is blind to the beloved's faults:

However, this love is not blind to the faults; it simply over-looks these perceived faults, or else does not regard them as shortcomings. Thus physical imperfections, as well as eco-nomic, educational, and social shortcomings, are far less important to healthy people than are character defects. As a consequence, it is easily possible for self-actualizing peo-ple to fall deeply in love with homely partners. This is called blindness by others, but it might much better be called good taste or perceptiveness. (M&P, 200-201)

SELF-ACTUALIZING SEX

"Self-actualizing persons often have ecstatic sex... [S]exual pleasures are found in their most intense and ecstatic perfection in self-actual-izing people." (M&P, 186-187) :

Finally, of course, there is a special sexual arousal in the lover. This, in the typical instance, shows itself directly in genital changes. The beloved person seems to have a special power that nobody else in the world has to the same degree of producing erection and secretion in the partner, of arousing specific conscious sexual desire, and of producing the usual pricklings and tinglings that go with sexual arousal. (M&P, 182)

HUMBLE CREATIVITY

Self-actualizing persons are creative in every avenue of life. This SA creativity is not the great talent kind of creativity such as that of a Mozart. It is more humble. We do not really understand the great talents, nor are they necessarily psychologically healthy:

> I first had to give up my stereotyped notion that health, genius, talent and productivity were synonymous. A fair proportion of my subjects … were not productive in the ordinary sense, nor did they have great talent or genius, nor were they poets, composers, inventors, artists or creative intellectuals. It was also obvious that some of the greatest talents of mankind were certainly not psychologically healthy people, Wagner, for example, or Van Gogh or Byron. (Being, 117)
>
> This [SA] creativeness appears in some of our subjects not in the usual forms of writing books, composing music, or producing artistic objects, but rather may be much more humble. It is as if this special type of creativeness … touches whatever activity the person is engaged in. In this sense there can be creative shoemakers or carpenters or clerks. (M&P, 171)

19

Some examples of self-actualizing creativity:

> [O]ne woman, uneducated, poor, a fulltime housewife and mother, did none of these conventionally creative things and yet was a marvelous cook, mother, wife and home-maker... She was in all these areas original, novel, ingenious, unexpected, inventive... I learned from her and others like her that a first-rate soup is more creative than a second-rate painting... (Being, 117)
>
> Another was a psychiatrist, a "pure" clinician who never wrote anything or created any theories or researches but who delighted in his everyday job of helping people to create themselves. This man approached each patient as if he were the only one in the world, without jargon, expectations or presuppositions, with innocence and naiveté and yet with great wisdom, in a Taoistic fashion. (Being, 117)
>
> From another man I learned that constructing a business organization could be a creative activity. From a young athlete, I learned that a perfect tackle could be as esthetic a product as a sonnet and could be approached in the same creative spirit. (Being, 117-118)

MORE SOCIALIZED AND MORE INDIVIDUALIZED

Self-actualizers "are more completely individual than any group that has ever been described, and yet are also more completely socialized, more identified with humanity than any other group yet described. They are closer to both their specieshood and to their unique individuality." (M&P, 178)

AFFECTION FOR HUMANKIND

Gemeinshaftgefühl is a word invented by Alfred Adler, which means a social or community feeling. It is:

> the only one available that describes well the flavor of the feelings for mankind expressed by self-actualizing subjects. They have for human beings in general a deep feeling of identification, sympathy, and affection in spite of the occasional anger, impatience, or disgust described below. Because of this they have a genuine desire to help the human race. (M&P, 165)

SELF-GOVERNING & DEMOCRATIC

Self-actualizing humans are autonomous, democratic self-starters. They are "ruled by the laws of their own character rather than by the rules of society." (M&P, 173-174) "All my subjects without exception may be said to be democratic people in the deepest possible sense … They can be and are friendly with anyone of suitable character regardless of class, education, political belief, race, or color." (M&P, 167)

TRANSCENDENCE OF SELFISHNESS AND UNSELFISHNESS

Despite the word "self" in self-actualizing persons, these individuals have transcended selfishness. They are both selfish and unselfish. Maslow commented: "I couldn't decide whether my subjects were selfish or unselfish." (Being, 120) It is as if the two qualities had fused into one, into some higher quality. "For self-actualizing people, there is a strong tendency for selfishness and unselfishness to fuse into a higher, superordinate unity." (Being, 170)

OTHER MEANINGS OF TRANSCENDENCE

Transcendence had many meanings for Maslow. Perhaps its core meaning is that of rising above the normal human experience, as happens in the peak experience (see below). It can refer to the fusion of opposite qualities, such as selfishness and unselfishness. It can also refer to transcendence of culture:

> Self-actualizing people have to a large extent transcended the values of their culture. They are not so much merely Americans as they are world citizens, members of the human species first and foremost. They are able to regard their own society objectively, liking some aspects of it, disliking others. (FR, 184)

For further information on Maslow's use of the term transcendence, see 'Transcendence and the Psychology of Being' in *The Farther Reaches of Human Nature*. See also Scott Kaufman's *Transcend*.

RESEMBLE RELIGIOUS SAINTS

Self-actualizing persons have some of the qualities of religious persons reported throughout history:

> [O]ur description of the actual characteristics of self-actualizing people parallels at many points the ideals urged by

the religions, e.g., the transcendence of self, the fusion of the true, the good and the beautiful, contribution to others, wisdom, honesty and naturalness, the transcendence of selfish and personal motivations, the giving up of "lower" desires in favor of "higher" ones, the easy differentiation between ends (tranquility, serenity, peace) and means (money, power, status), the decrease of hostility, cruelty and destructiveness and the increase of friendliness, kindness, etc. (Being, 134)

IV. Peak Experiences

SOME OR MOST PEOPLE have mystical experiences, which Maslow called peak experiences. These are moments when daily life recedes and the person may feel ecstatic:

> [There were] feelings of limitless horizons opening up to the vision, the feeling of being simultaneously more powerful and also more helpless than one ever was before, the feeling of great ecstasy and wonder and awe, the loss of placing in time and space with, finally, the conviction that something extremely important and valuable had happened, so that the subject is to some extent transformed and strengthened even in his daily life by such experiences. (M&P, 164)

At first Maslow confined his study of peak experiences to self-actualizers, and made a distinction between those who had peak experiences and those who did not:

> [T]he nonpeaking self-actualizers seem so far to tend to be practical, effective people… Peakers seem also to live in the realm of Being; of poetry, esthetics; symbols; transcendence; "religion" of the mystical, personal, noninstitutional sort; and of end experiences… [I]t looks as though the "merely healthy" nonpeaking self-actualizers seem likely to be the social world improvers, the politicians, the workers in society, the reformers, the crusaders, whereas the transcending peakers are more apt to write the poetry, the music, the philosophies, and the religions. (M&P, 165)

As Maslow grew more skillful at interrogating his subjects, he discovered that most if not all persons, at all levels of the hierarchy of needs, seem to have peak experiences:

> I finally began to use the word "nonpeaker" to describe, not the person who is unable to have peak-experiences, but rather the person who is afraid of them, who suppresses them, who denies them, who turns away from them, or who "forgets" them. (Religion, 37)

Maslow would go on to examine religion in the light of peak experiences. See *Religion* below.

V. Human Values

FAILURE OF TRADITIONAL VALUE SYSTEMS

PART OF MASLOW'S MOTIVATION in investigating human behavior was the collapse of traditional value systems in the twentieth century. "These agreed-upon traditions are all gone. Of course, we never should have rested on tradition... It was destroyed too easily by truth, by honesty, by the facts, by science, by simple, pragmatic, historical failure." (Religion, 23)

Our faith in progress "died with World War I, with Freud, with the depression, with the atom bomb." (Religion, 53)

Attempts to create humanistic value systems have also all failed:

> Humanists for thousands of years have attempted to construct a naturalistic, psychological value system that could be derived from man's own nature, without the necessity of recourse to authority outside the human being himself. Many such theories have been offered throughout history ... Today practically all of these can be shown, in the light of recently acquired knowledge, to be false, inadequate, incomplete or in some other way, lacking. (Being, 127)

ANIMAL STUDIES

Animal studies also do not provide human values: "Too many of the findings that have been made in animals have been proved to be true for animals but not for the human being." (M&P, 56) "It is no more necessary to study animals before one can study man than it is to study mathematics before one can study geology or psychology or biology." (M&P, 56)

A VALUE SYSTEM BASED ON HUMAN NEEDS

The true human value system lies in the hierarchy of needs. A "hierarchy of human values" is "to be found in the very essence of human nature itself. These are not only wanted and desired by all human beings, but also needed in the sense that they are necessary to avoid illness and psychopathology." (M&P, xiii)

> It is these needs, "instinctoid" in nature, that we can also think of as built-in values — values not only in the sense that the organism wants and seeks them but also in the sense that they are both good and necessary for the organism. (Science, 68)

THE BEING-VALUES

Once the lower needs are met, the self-actualizing person is motivated by such values as goodness, truth, beauty, justice, and completeness. Maslow calls these the *Being-values*, or *B-values*, for short. "Self-actualizing people ... seem to do what they do for the sake of ultimate, final values... Self-actualizing people are motivated by the eternal verities, the B-Values, by pure truth and beauty in perfection." (FR, 192-193)

The B-values are not in a hierarchy; instead, they are like the several facets of a single gem. "One is as important as the next, and each one can be defined in terms of all the others ... The B-Values are not separate piles of sticks, but rather the different facets of one jewel." (FR, 194)

The B-values act as needs which must be satisfied. "For the self-actualizing human the B-values are needs. If they are not satisfied, the human can become sick: sicknesses of the soul." (FR, 44)

THE BEING-VALUES REPRESENT TRUE HUMANITY

Maslow thought that the Being-values could be used as a value system for all humanity. Being-values reveal more of the original nature of the human species than do the values of neurotic persons.

> Could these self-actualizing people be more human, more revealing of the original nature of the species, closer to the species type in the taxonomical sense? Ought a biological species to be judged by its crippled, warped, only partially developed specimens, or by examples that have been overdomesticated, caged, and trained? (M&P, 159)

"[T]he study of crippled, stunted, immature, and unhealthy specimens can yield only a crippled psychology and a crippled philosophy. The study of self-actualizing people must be the basis for a more universal science of psychology." (M&P, 180)

These being-values are biological, not divine, in origin:

> [T]hese propositions affirm the existence of the highest values within human nature itself, to be discovered there. This is in sharp contradiction to the older and more customary

beliefs that the highest values can come only from a super-natural God. (Being, 160)

HUMAN NEEDS ARE HUMAN RIGHTS

Every human has needs that must be met, therefore they should be considered human rights:

> [I]t is legitimate and fruitful to regard instinctoid basic needs and the metaneeds as rights… [H]uman beings have a right to be human in the same sense that cats have a right to be cats. In order to be fully human, these need and metaneed gratifications are necessary, and may therefore be considered to be natural rights. (M&P, xiii)

VI. How To?

HOW DO YOU GO ABOUT satisfying your basic needs? How do you self-actualize?

SOCIETY AND RELATIONSHIPS

Basic needs, from physiological to esteem, can only be gratified by other people, that is, society.

> [B]asic human needs can be fulfilled only by and through other human beings, i.e., society. The need for community (belongingness, contact, groupiness) is itself a basic need ... And of course it has also been known for decades that humanness and specieshood in the infant are only a potentiality and must be actualized by the society. (Religion, 10)

"Any ultimate analysis of human, interpersonal relationships, e.g., friendship, marriage, etc., will show that basic needs can be satisfied only interpersonally ... namely, the giving of safety, love, belongingness, feeling of worth, and self-esteem." (M&P, 248)

"Just as all trees need sun, water, and foods from the environment, so do all people need safety, love and status from their environment." (Being, 36)

LIFE EXPERIENCES

Good life experiences can help with growth.

> For cases that are young enough, and that are not too seri-
> ous, a good marriage, success in a suitable job, developing
> good friendships, having children, facing emergencies, and
> overcoming difficulties—I have occasionally seen all of these
> produce deep character changes, get rid of symptoms, etc.
> without the help of a technical therapist. As a matter of fact,
> a case could be made for the thesis that good life circum-
> stances are among the ultimate therapeutic agents and that
> technical psychotherapy often has the task only of enabling
> the individual to take advantage of them. (M&P, 246)

PEAK EXPERIENCES

Peak experiences can permanently enhance psychological health:
"Sometimes their after-effects are so profound and so great as to
remind us of the profound religious conversions which forever after
changed the person." (Religion, 92)

THERAPY

Many people have ungratified basic needs. Here therapy is the main
helpful intervention:

> As a result of successful psychotherapy, people perceive dif-
> ferently, think differently, learn differently. Their motives

change, as do their emotions. It is the best technique we have ever had for laying bare men's deepest nature as contrasted with their surface personalities. Their interpersonal relations and attitudes toward society are transformed. Their characters (or personalities) change both superficially and profoundly. There is even some evidence that their appearance changes, that physical health is improved, etc. In some cases, even the IQ goes up. (M&P, 241)

"[P]rofessional psychotherapists every day, as a matter of course, change and improve human nature, help people to become more strong, virtuous, creative, kind, loving, altruistic, serene." (Being, 139)

Unfortunately, there are not enough therapists to go around, nor are all humans amenable to therapy:

I gave up long ago improving the whole human species via individual psychology. This is impracticable. As a matter of fact it is impossible quantitatively. (Especially in view of the fact that so many people are not suitable for individual psychotherapy.) (EM, 1)

GROUP THERAPY

Group therapy can reach more people at one time.

"If ordinary therapy may be conceived of as a miniature ideal society of two, then group therapy may be seen as a miniature ideal society of ten."

These groups take many forms: "T-groups, basic encounter groups, sensitivity training, and all the other kinds of groups now categorized as personal growth groups or affective education semi-nars and workshops."

Group therapy has the same goals as individual therapy.

"Though quite different in procedure, they may yet be said to have the same far goals of all psychotherapies, that is, self-actualiza-tion, full-humanness, fuller use of species and personal potentials, etc." (M&P, 263-264)

EDUCATION AND WORKPLACE

Looking at society, Maslow identified two places where good con-ditions could affect most humans: education and the workplace. In *Part II* below, we will examine these two potential avenues of growth.

VII. Limits to Growth

SOME PEOPLE CANNOT HAVE their basic needs gratified, for various reasons.

Some are too psychologically ill:

> As [psychological] illness becomes more and more severe, it becomes less and less accessible to benefit from need gratification. There comes a point in this continuum where (1) basic need gratifications are often not even sought for or wanted, having been given up in favor of neurotic-need gratifications, and (2) even when they are offered, the patient cannot use them. It is no use offering him affection, for he is afraid of it, mistrusts it, misinterprets it, and finally refuses it. (M&P, 258)

Similarly, "[I]n the psychopathic personality the needs for being loved and loving have disappeared, and so far as we know today, this is usually a permanent loss..." (M&P, 84)

Some respond poorly to good conditions:

> [G]ood conditions, though they have a growth effect on most of the population, nevertheless also have a bad, even catastrophic, effect on a certain small proportion of the population. Freedom and trust given to authoritarians, for instance, will simply bring out bad behavior in these people. Freedom and permissiveness and responsibility will make really dependent and passive people collapse in anxiety and fear. (EM, 243)

Moreover, even those who could grow often refuse to:

> Throughout history, learned men have set out before man-
> kind the rewards of virtue, the beauties of goodness, the
> intrinsic desirability of psychological health and self-fulfill-
> ment, and yet most people perversely refuse to step into the
> happiness and self-respect that is offered them. (Being, 139)

"Not only do we hang on to our psychopathology, but also we tend to
evade personal growth..." (Being, 58)

Also, people can be afraid of their higher nature: "It is precisely
the god-like in ourselves that we are ambivalent about, fascinated by
and fearful of, motivated to and defensive against." (Being, 59)

Growth is difficult: "Self-knowledge and self-improvement is
very difficult for most people. It usually needs great courage and long
struggle." (Being, 139)

> Growth has not only rewards and pleasures but also intrinsic
> pains. Each step forward is a step into the unfamiliar. Growth
> also means giving up something familiar and good and satis-
> fying. It means giving up a simpler and easier and less effort-
> ful life, in exchange for a more demanding, more responsible,
> more difficult life. Growth in spite of these losses therefore
> requires courage, will, choice, and strength in the individ-
> ual... (Being, 168)

The result of the refusal to grow can be that the person decides to live
at a lower level of the hierarchy of needs. (FR, 249)

Even the healthiest people are not completely healthy.

There are no perfect human beings! Persons can be found who are good, very good indeed, in fact, great. There do in fact exist creators, seers, sages, saints, shakers, and movers. This can certainly give us hope for the future of the species even if they are uncommon and do not come by the dozen. And yet these very same people can at times be boring, irritating, petulant, selfish, angry, or depressed. To avoid disillusionment with human nature, we must first give up our illusions about it. (M&P, 176)

TWO

*Social Implications
of the Theory of Human Nature*

MASLOW APPLIED HIS THEORY of human nature to various aspects of society: education, the workplace, religion, science, and politics. In general, he was searching for ways to improve psychological health in individuals.

VIII. Education

MASLOW WAS HIGHLY critical of American education, and suggested ways to improve it in line with his theory of human nature. "Our conventional education looks mighty sick." (FR, 184)

GOAL OF EDUCATION

The far goal of education should be psychological growth, that is, gratification of needs and self-actualization.

> [T]he far goal of education as of psychotherapy, of family life, of work, of society, of life itself—is to aid the person to grow to fullest humanness, to the greatest fulfillment and actualization of his highest potentials, to his greatest possible stature...to become the best he is capable of becoming, to become actually what he deeply is potentially. (Religion, 66-67)

"Education must be seen as at least partially an effort to produce the good human being, to foster the good life and the good society." (Religion, 76)

PASSING ON KNOWLEDGE IS NOT EDUCATION

The passing on of knowledge does not contribute to growth toward full humanness.

"Much that we have called learning has become useless... Education can no longer be considered essentially or only a learning process; it is now also a character training, a person-training process." (FR, 99)

Information by itself will not change the world.

> What is wrong is not the great discoveries of science-information is always better than ignorance, no matter what information or what ignorance. What is wrong is the belief behind the information, the belief that information will change the world. It won't. (Archibald MacLeish, quoted in FR, 171)

"How did my trigonometry course help me to become a better human being?" ... "By gosh, it didn't!" (FR, 184)

ACQUISITION OF SKILLS IS NOT EDUCATION

Teaching skills is more aptly called technical training, which can be taught about the same way in either democratic or authoritarian societies.

> If one took a course or picked up a book on the psychology of learning, most of it, in my opinion, would be beside the point - that is, beside the "humanistic" point. Most of it would present learning as the acquisition of associations, of skills and capacities that are external and not intrinsic to the human character, to the human personality, to the person himself. (FR, 168)

INTRINSIC EDUCATION: IDENTITY

What we need instead is intrinsic education, which helps students find their identity. Intrinsic education is "learning to be a human being in general, and second, learning to be this particular human being." (FR, 170)

> You are learning what you peculiarly are, how you are you, what your potentialities are, what your style is, what your pace is, what your tastes are, what your values are, what direction your body is going, where your personal biology is taking you, i.e, how you are different from others. (FR, 187)

For intrinsic education the arts are more helpful than the core curriculum:

> [E]ffective education in music, education in art, education in dancing and rhythm, is intrinsically far closer than the usual "core curriculum" to intrinsic education of the kind that I am talking about, of learning one's identity as an essential part of education. If education doesn't do that, it is useless. Education is learning to grow, learning what to grow toward, learning what is good and bad, learning what is desirable and undesirable, learning what to choose and what not to choose ... [T]he arts, and especially the ones that I have mentioned, are so close to our psychological and biological core, ... that rather than think of these courses as a sort of whipped cream or luxury, they must become basic experiences in education. (FR, 173)

ABRAHAM H. MASLOW

INTRINSIC EDUCATION:
GRATIFICATION OF NEEDS

"Another important goal of intrinsic education is to see that the child's basic psychological needs are satisfied. A child cannot reach self-actualization until his needs for security, belongingness, dignity, love, respect, and esteem are all satisfied." (FR, 190)

> Whether character education can take place in the class-room, whether books, lectures, catechisms, and exhorta-tions are the best tools to use, whether sermons and Sunday schools can produce good human beings, or rather whether the good life produces the good man, whether love, warmth, friendship, respect, and good treatment of the child are more consequential for his later character structure—these are the alternatives presented by adherence to one or the other the-ory of character formation and of education. (M&P, 66)

TEACHING OF VALUES

To teach school children the B-values would transform society. Such teaching need not violate separation of church and state.

> [T]he teaching of spiritual values, of ethical and moral values definitely does (in principle) have a place in education, per-haps ultimately a very basic and essential place... this in no way needs to controvert the American separation between church and state for the very simple reason that spiritual, ethical, and moral values ... are the common core of all

44

churches… We reject the notion of distant value-goals in education under the penalty of falling into the great danger of defining education as mere technological training without relation to the good life, to ethics, to morals, or for that matter to anything else. (Religion, 76)

"If we were to accept as a major educational goal the awakening and fulfillment of the B-Values … People would be stronger, healthier, and would take their own lives into their hands to a greater extent." (FR, 195)

PEAK EXPERIENCES IN EDUCATION

Peak experiences are tremendously useful in learning, but the emphasis on order in our classrooms crushes them.

> I think it is possible to think of the peak experience, the experience of awe, mystery, wonder, or of perfect completion, as the goal and reward of learning as well … If this is true for the great historians, mathematicians, scientists, musicians, philosophers, and all the rest, why should we not try to maximize these studies as sources of peak experiences for the child as well? (FR, 190)
>
> [T]he present school system is an extremely effective instrument for crushing peak experiences and forbidding their possibility … Of course, with the traditional model of thirty-five children in one classroom and a curriculum of subject matter which has to be gotten through in a given period of time, the teacher is forced to pay more attention to

orderliness and lack of noise than she is making learning a joyful experience. (FR, 188)

DELIGHT IN EDUCATION

Delight is an integral part of education, because it is the main guide in finding your way to your own identity:

> [T]he child must be permitted to retain the subjective experiences of delight and boredom, as the criteria of the correct choice for him. The alternative criterion is making the choice in terms of the wish of another person. The Self is lost when this happens. (Being, 54)

The "notion of growth-through-delight" ties in nicely "with all the dynamic theories of Freud, Adler, Jung, Schachtel, Horney, Fromm and Rank, as well as The Self theories of Rogers, Bühler, Combs, Angyal, Allport, Goldstein and of the Growth-and-Being school, Dewey, Rasey, Kelley, Moustakas, Wilson, Perls, Lee, Mearns, etc." (Being, 48)

SCIENCE EDUCATION: SEE FOR YOURSELF

The root of science is "see for yourself."

"One of the beginnings of science, one of the roots from which it grew, was the determination not to take things on faith, trust, logic, or authority but to check and to see for oneself. (Science, 40)

This should be taught to school children.

"It is this empirical attitude that I claim can and should be taught to all human beings, including young children. Look for yourself! Let's see how it works! Is that claim correct? How correct?" (Science, 74)

LIFE EXPERIENCES

Life experiences also can provide education toward full humanness.

> In my life such experiences have been far more important than classes, listening to lectures, memorizing the branches of the twelve cranial nerves and dissecting a human brain, or memorizing the insertions of the muscles, or the kinds of things that one does in medical schools, in biology courses, or other such courses." (FR, 169)
>
> Far more important for me have been such experiences as having a child. Our first baby changed me as a psychologist. It made the behaviorism I had been so enthusiastic about look so foolish that I could not stomach it any more. It was impossible, having a second baby, and learning how profoundly different people are even before birth, made it impossible for me to think in terms of the kind of learning psychology in which one can teach anybody anything. (FR, 169)

"[G]etting married ... was certainly far more important than my Ph.D. by way of instructiveness." (FR, 170)

IX. Workplace

Since almost everybody works, good conditions in the workplace can assist almost everybody in their psychological growth.

"Only recently has it dawned on me that as important as education, perhaps even more important, is the work life of the individual since everybody works." (EM, 2)

Good conditions at work can help not only the individual but also the firm. "[Good] conditions of work are often good not only for personal fulfillment, but also for the health and prosperity of the organization, as well as for the quantity and quality of the products or services turned out by the organization." (FR, 404)

"[P]ractically all the utopian ... and ethical and moral recommendations that must be made for such an enterprise will improve everything, and this includes profits..." (EM, 41)

GOAL OF THE WORKPLACE

Therefore, the far goal of any workplace ought to be the psychological health of its employees.

> Just as it's possible to say bluntly and unmistakably that the purpose or far goal of all psychotherapy is growth toward self-actualization..., so also can we say that this is ... also the far goal of any enlightened work enterprise... (EM, 39)

THE GOOD MANAGER

Psychologically healthier people make better managers. They improve the health of their workers, and they improve the performance of their workgroups.

> It was found, for instance, in Jim Clark's studies or in many of the studies quoted in the Likert book that one department was doing better economically than another department, that is, it had a higher production rate or it had less turnover or it had better morale or something of this sort, and the experiment was made in order to find out what factors were responsible for this economic superiority.
>
> What was found in practically all of these cases was that a particular kind of foreman or supervisor-manager was responsible for the economic superiority of the working group. And the qualities of the superior managers have been worked out, i.e., they are more democratic, more compassionate, more friendly, more helpful, more loyal, etc., etc. ... [A] certain kind of democratic manager makes more profit for the firm as well as making everybody happier and healthier. (EM, 82-83)

TRYING TO BE A GOOD MANAGER

Trying to become a good manager may not give the same results as being "intuitively and unconsciously" a good manager. Maslow relates the evidence of superior and inferior chickens:

49

> In Dove's experiments on superior chickens, "the superiors were found to be superior in every way, i.e., they had healthier feathers and healthier combs, they laid better eggs and more of them, they were heavier and stronger, they were higher in the pecking order, and they chose spontaneously … a better diet for physical health… When this dietary which was chosen by the superior chickens was forced upon the inferior chickens, these inferior chickens improved in all the mentioned qualities… That is, they got heavier and they laid better eggs; they rose in the pecking hierarchy and they had more sexual contacts, etc. But they never rose as high in these qualities as the innately superior chickens. They went about 50 percent of the way up. (EM, 82)

Similarly, in management:

> Anybody who puts on behavior like a cloak, as an actor would, finds that this doesn't work very well. People somehow are able to detect at some conscious or unconscious level that a person is acting and not really feeling deeply the attitude which he is trying to convey through his behavior. So in the same way we have the possible complication that the supervisor who takes all sorts of courses and reads all sorts of books and is trained in various ways and who agrees with the data and who honestly tries to behave like a superior supervisor, may not be able to get the same results if he does not deeply feel democratic, parental, affectionate, etc. (EM, 85)

"And yet what else is possible?"

"There is no way for an authoritarian supervisor to become a democratic supervisor except by passing through the transitional stage of consciously, artificially, voluntarily trying to be a democratic supervisor." (EM, 86)

THEORY X, THEORY Y, THEORY Z

Douglas McGregor coined the terms Theory X and Theory Y to describe two different styles of management, a more autocratic and a more humanistic style. Maslow aligned Theory Y with self-actualizing persons who did not have peak experiences. Maslow then went on to postulate a Theory Z, which aligned with self-actualizing persons who did have peak experiences. (See 'Theory Z' in FR, 280 ff)

DEMOCRACY IN THE WORKPLACE

Good conditions in the workplace are essential to a democratic society.

> If democratic, political philosophy means anything at all, then enlightened management can be considered under the head of democratic philosophy applied to the work situation. (EM, 61)
>
> [D]emocracy needs absolutely for its very existence people who can think for themselves, make their own judgments, and finally, who can vote for themselves—that is, who can rule themselves and help to rule their own country. Authoritarian enterprises do just the opposite of this; democracies do exactly just this. The best way to destroy democratic society would be by way of not only political authoritarianism but of industrial authoritarianism, which is anti-democratic in the deepest

sense. Therefore, any man who really wants to help his country, who is devoted to it, and who would sacrifice for it and take upon his own shoulders the responsibility for its improvement, must, if he is to be logical, carry this whole philosophy into his work life. (EM, 61-62)

BAD REACTIONS TO GOOD CONDITIONS

Like people in general (see *Limits to Growth* above), some workers may not respond well to good conditions and, in fact, may be hurt by them.

> They may get by in the ordinary authoritarian, conventional structure situation, but in the free and open and self-responsible situation, they discover that they are, e.g., not really interested in working, or that they mistrust their intelligence, or that they may become overwhelmed by depression which they have been strongly repressing, etc. What this means for organization theorists is that in all their calculations in moving over to the newer style of management, they should assume that a certain proportion-as yet unknown-will not respond well to good conditions. (EM, 43)

Not everybody is motivated to participate in management:

> We don't know how many people or what proportion of the working population would actually prefer to participate in management decisions, and how many would prefer not to have anything to do with them. What proportion of the

population take a job as simply any old kind of a job which they must do in order to earn a living, while their interests are very definitely centered outside of the job. (EM, 54)

Example:

> [A] woman who works only because she has to support her children. It's perfectly true that she'll prefer a nice and pleasant job to a rotten job... How much involvement does she really want in the enterprise if the center of her life is definitely in her children rather than in her job?

Also:

> What proportion of the population prefer authoritarian bosses, prefer to be told what to do, don't want to bother thinking, etc.? What proportion of the population is reduced to the concrete and so finds planning for the future totally incomprehensible and boring? ... We know very little about physical inertia or psychic inertia. How lazy are people and under what circumstances and what makes them not lazy? We just don't know. (EM, 54)

"Some people may not have a "feeling for workmanship..." (EM, 53)

HYPOTHESIS NOT DOGMA

There is a tendency to treat social theories as eternal truths. Instead, they should be seen as hypotheses, in the scientific sense, therefore requiring verification. What will work in a given work situation is a matter for investigation.

> This is what I get vaguely uneasy about in the reading on management, namely a certain piety, certain semi-religious attitudes, an unthinking, unreasoning, a priori kind of "liberalism" which frequently takes over as a determinant, thereby to some extent destroying the possibility of maintaining the necessary sensitivity to the objective requirements of the actual, realistic situation. (EM, 71)
>
> I detect a certain doctrinaire quality in much of the writing about growth or enlightened management policy. So many of the writers talk as if this new management policy were "good" in some platonic sense, in an absolute way. That is, the implication is that it's always good. And therefore there is a neglect of the circumstances in which these policies are to be applied. Or to put it in another way, the point tends to be lost that good management policies are pragmatically good, good in a functional sense, that they produce better results than the older style of management. That is, for the moment, they are not to be considered good in themselves, intrinsically, because God said so, but rather because they work better, they justify their existence in terms of increased productivity, or better quality of product, or greater growth of democratic citizens, etc. (EM, 70)

"The kind of management policy which is best in each of these situations is that policy which will work best. In order to find out what this is, a full objectivity is required without a priori presuppositions or pious expectations." (EM, 73)

X. Society

MASLOW'S APPLIED HIS THEORY of human nature to a variety of societal topics.

BAD AND GOOD ANIMALS

At the heart of Western societal thinking has been the belief that humans are bad.

> For inscrutable reasons that only the intellectual historian may be able to unravel, western civilization has generally believed that the animal in us was a bad animal, and that our most primitive impulses are evil, greedy, selfish, and hostile. The theologians have called it original sin, or the devil. The Freudians have called it id … (M&P, 82-83)

This evil nature was said to be best exemplified in sick human beings.

> Coordinate with the bad-animal interpretation of instincts was the expectation that they would be seen most clearly in the insane, the neurotic, the criminal, the feeble-minded, or the desperate. This follows naturally from the doctrine that conscience, rationality, and ethics are no more than an acquired veneer, completely different in character from what lies beneath, and are related to that underneath as manacles to prisoner. (M&P, 86)

If humans are bad animals, then society's function is restraint. "As a consequence, many cultural institutions are set up for the express purpose of controlling, inhibiting, suppressing and repressing this original nature of man." (Being, 138)

> This mistake is so crucial, so tragedy laden… Any belief that makes men mistrust themselves and each other unnecessarily, and to be unrealistically pessimistic about human possibilities, must be held partly responsible for every war that has ever been waged, for every racial antagonism, and for every religious massacre. (M&P, 86)

Contrary to the bad animal view, it has now been shown that human nature is essentially good.

> While it is still necessary to be very cautious about affirming the preconditions for "goodness" in human nature, it is already possible to reject firmly the despairing belief that human nature is ultimately and basically depraved and evil. Such a belief is no longer a matter of taste merely. It can now be maintained only by a determined blindness and ignorance, by a refusal to consider the facts. (M&P, x-xi)

THE PURPOSE OF THE GOOD SOCIETY

We have seen that basic human needs can only be gratified by society. Therefore, it is the purpose of society to fulfill these needs. In fact, we may define the *good society* as one that satisfies human needs.

> (1) since a man is to be called sick who is basically thwarted, and (2) since such basic thwarting is made possible ultimately

only by forces outside the individual, then (3) sickness in the individual must come ultimately from a sickness in the society. The good or healthy society would then be defined as one that permitted man's highest purposes to emerge by satisfying all his basic needs. (M&P, 58)

The good society is:

> one that gives to its members the greatest possibility of becoming sound and self-actualizing human beings. This in turn means that the good society is the one that has its institutional arrangements set up in such a way as to foster, encourage, reward, produce a maximum of good human relationships and a minimum of bad human relationships. (M&P, 255)

"The purpose or far goal of any good society is growth toward self-actualization." (EM, 39)

FREEDOM TO SELF-ACTUALIZE

Once a person's basic needs are gratified, however, it is essential that society step back to provide the individual the freedom to self-actualize.

> From the point of view of fostering self-actualization, a good environment is one that offers all necessary raw materials and then gets out of the way to let the organism itself utter its wishes and demands and make its choices... (M&P, 277)

Society cannot help the person to self-actualize. "In the later stages of growth the person is essentially alone and can rely only upon himself." (Being, 40)

Any direction the society gives to self-actualization may actually damage the individual.

"[H]uman nature is extremely malleable in the sense that it is easy for culture and environment to kill off altogether or to diminish genetic potential, although it cannot create or even increase this potential." (M&P, xviii)

Individuality in particular is "very plastic, superficial, easily changed, easily stamped out, but producing thereby all sorts of subtle pathologies." (M&P, xviii)

WAYS TO IMPROVE SOCIETY

IMPROVE HUMAN BEINGS

As human beings become psychologically healthier, in turn they improve society.

> The pursuit and the gratification of the higher needs have desirable civic and social consequences ... People who have enough basic satisfaction ... tend to develop such qualities as loyalty, friendliness, and civic consciousness, and to become better parents, husbands, teachers, public servants... (M&P, 99-100)

In particular, self-actualizing persons are our best reformers.

The empirical fact is that self-actualizing people, our best experiencers, are also our most compassionate, our great improvers and reformers of society, our most effective fighters against injustice, inequality, slavery, cruelty, exploitation (and also our best fighters for excellence, effectiveness, competence). (Religion, 9)

THERAPY

Because therapy improves human beings, it can be seen as a revolutionary technique to improve society, as well.

[I]f psychotherapy could be tremendously extended... That the society would change there can be no doubt. First would come changes here and there in the flavor of human relationships with respect to such qualities as hospitality, generosity, friendliness, and the like, but when enough people became more hospitable, more generous, more kind, more social, then we may rest assured that they would force legal, political, economic, and sociological changes as well. (M&P, 256)

[N]o matter what the degree of general health or sickness of a society, therapy amounts to fighting against the sickness-producing forces in that society on an individual scale. It tries, so to speak, to turn the tide, to bore from within, to be revolutionary or radical... (M&P, 256)

"[T]herapy may be phrased as an attempt to set up a miniature good society." (M&P, 256)

GOOD WORKPLACES
AND INTRINSIC EDUCATION

We have seen that good workplaces improve individual health; they thereby improve society. "[P]roper management of the work lives of human beings, of the way in which they earn their living, can improve them and improve the world and in this sense be a utopian or revolutionary technique." (EM, 1)

Similarly: "If we were to accept as a major educational goal the awakening and fulfillment of the B-Values we would have a great flowering of a new kind of civilization." (FR, 195)

SYNERGY

THE GOOD PERSON AND THE GOOD SOCIETY

As we have seen, there is a chicken and egg aspect to improving individual health and societal health. The good society improves the individual, and in return the good individual improves the society.

"The first and overarching Big Problem is to make the Good Person." ... "The equally Big Problem as urgent as the one I have already mentioned is to make the Good Society." (FR, 19)

> There is a kind of a feedback between the Good Society and the Good Person. They need each other, they are *sine qua non* to each other. I wave aside the problem of which comes first. It is quite clear that they develop simultaneously and in tandem. It would in any case be impossible to achieve one without the other. (FR, 19)

One way the good person and the good society are related is via the social arrangement of synergy. It was Ruth Benedict who created the anthropological concept of synergy. Her findings were never published, but her student Maslow reconstructed them from his notes.

Benedict was trying to create a comparative sociology of indigenous cultures. She constructed two sets of four cultures each, then struggled to find the right way to differentiate them. One set was surly and the other was nice. One set was anxious, and the other not. One set was low morale and the other was high morale. One set was full of hatred and aggression, and the other of affection. One set was insecure and the other was secure. Benedict "tried one after another all the generalizations…, all the standard canopeners, you might call them, that were available at that time. She compared them on the basis of race, geography, climate, size." She examined suicide rates, polygamy, matrilineal versus patrilineal, big houses and small houses, rich or poor. Each of these criteria failed to differentiate the secure cultures from the insecure ones.

Finally, Benedict realized that the difference between the two sets of cultures lay in their social arrangements. In the bad cultures the social arrangement set people against each other. In the good cultures the most successful people who sought their own selfish good simultaneously helped other members of the society. In the bad cultures the wealthy became wealthier, and the poor poorer. In the good cultures wealth tended to flow from rich to poor; it was spread around. Benedict chose the terms "high synergy" and "low synergy" to describe the two sets of cultures. (FR, 199 ff)

"Those societies have high synergy in which the social institutions are set up so as to transcend the polarity between selfishness and unselfishness, between self-interest and altruism ..." (FR, 202)

Maslow did field work among the Blackfoot Indians. He considered them a classic example of synergy. Among the Blackfoot the wealthiest person is the one who amasses the most wealth during the year and then gives it all away at the annual Sun Dance ceremony. "The people most respected in this tribe are the people who have given away most." Afterwards, he has such prestige that everyone in the tribe fights for his presence. "He is regarded as so wise that to have him at the fireplace where he can teach the children is regarded as a great blessing. In this way he benefits and everyone benefits from his skill, his intelligence, his hard work, his generosity." (EM, 20-21)

The possibility of synergy means that it is a mistake to regard society and the individual as necessarily antagonistic. "We can now reject ... the almost universal mistake that the interests of the individual and of society are *of necessity* mutually exclusive and antagonistic, or that civilization is primarily a mechanism for controlling and policing human instinctoid impulses." (Being, 134)

A healthy society is a synergetic society. "Individual and social interests under healthy social conditions are synergic and not antagonistic." (M&P, 85)

We can consciously use the concept of synergy in the design of organizations, "so that the goals of the individual merge with the goals of the organization." (FR, 237)

EUPSYCHIA

Maslow imagined a psychological utopia called Eupsychia. He envisioned a hundred healthy families in a deserted land. Their culture would permit people to make free choices whenever possible. People would be far less controlling, violent, contemptuous, or overbearing. They would be much less likely to press their opinions or religions or philosophies or tastes on their neighbors. Under such conditions, the deepest layers of human nature could show themselves with greater ease. (M&P, 277-278)

The key points to this ideal society are these: First, everyone is assumed psychologically healthy. Second, each person is given extreme freedom of choice to follow their individual nature to self-actualization.

EUPSYCHIAN AS AN ADJECTIVE

As an adjective eupsychian need not describe a Eupsychia, it can also serve as a synonym for the good society or for good conditions. It can mean moving toward psychological health. (EM, xi)

UTOPIA VERSUS EUPSYCHIA

Maslow distinguished between a typical utopia and a Eupsychia. A typical utopia is a fantasy; it projects certainty, inevitability, and perfectibility. It is dogmatic. By contrast, a Eupsychia is based upon science. The classic questions would then be posed as research questions and investigated:

"How good a society does human nature permit?"

"How good a human nature does society permit?"

"How good a society does the nature of society permit?" (EM, xi)

NO PERFECT SOCIETY

There will never be a perfect society:

> [N]o society, however good, could completely eliminate sickness. If threats do not come from other human beings, they will always come from nature, from death, from frustration, from sickness, even from the mere fact that by living together in a society, though we advantage ourselves thereby, we must also necessarily modify the form of satisfying our desires. Nor dare we forget that human nature itself generates much evil, if not from inborn malice, then from ignorance, stupidity, fear, miscommunications, clumsiness, etc. (M&P, 257)

There will always remain some violent persons: "In the most peaceful of societies, with the most perfect social and economic conditions, some people will have to be violent just because of the way they are constructed." (M&P, 128)

There will always be conflict: "The short and sure path to despair and surrender is this, to believe that there is somewhere a scheme of things that will eliminate conflict, struggle, stupidity, cupidity, personal jealousy." (David Ulienthall, quoted in FR, 227-8)

THE SLOW REVOLUTION

To create Eupsychia, there must be a revolution. The revolution must occur first in human nature: No "social reforms, no beautiful constitutions or beautiful programs or laws will be of any consequence unless people are healthy enough, evolved enough, strong enough, good enough to understand them and to want to put them into practice in the right way." (FR, 19)

This new revolution must be a slow one, guided by science: We must accept "the necessity and the inevitability of slow rather than rapid social change." (EM, 248) "We must have the patience of the scientist who waits until the data are in before he draws his conclusions." (EM, 260)

> The scientific attitude that is needed is, and must be, very pervasive and very deep. That is, every suggested improvement ought to be considered a hypothesis or an experiment to be tested and confirmed, always with the implication that it may turn out to be untrue or false or unwise... (EM, 258)

Revolutionaries in this revolution forego violence: "[T]he people who work at social betterment must be a very different kind of revolutionary from any that have existed. They must accept fully and understand fully and even approve of the necessity for slow rather than rapid change." (EM, 248)

"This is a shiftover from the traditional revolutionary requirement of people who are ready to fight and to kill." (EM, 249)

There must be a broad advance on all fronts: There must be a "slow holistic revolution by simultaneous attack along the total front, with conscious and controlled knowledge, and infiltration at the weakest or readiest points." (EM, 250)

> [Y]ou can't improve any society by pushing a single button or by making a single law or changing a single institution or having a particular kind of change in regime or leader or

president or dictator or whatever the case may be. I know of no single change that will automatically transform the whole society. (EM, 247)

Every job in this revolution is important:

> [T]here must be a division of labor in the task of changing a society, that is to say, there must necessarily be many people and many kinds of people to do the job. And this means in turn that each of these people is as necessary as any of the other individuals. Every kind of character, every kind of skill, every kind of talent, every kind of genius can be used and must be used, as a matter of fact is a prerequisite to total social change. (EM, 253-4)

"In ideal social change everybody is a general. ... [I]t then becomes quite possible and feasible for any person to do anything that needs doing and feel good about it." (EM, 254)

Each person does "that at which he can be better than anybody else in the whole world." (EM, 254)

Little tasks are prerequisite to bigger tasks. (EM, 252)

> Applied to the industrial situation ... a multitude of little steps, little committee meetings, and little conversations are necessary before a particular plant can make its transition over from a lower-need motivational level, or authoritarian level to a higher basic need level or to democratic or enlightened management level. Each of these little steps is absolutely necessary and each of them is doing a big job. Or to say it in another way, any big job like improving American

industry, translates itself down to millions of little jobs. There
is no big job other than the total sum of all these little jobs.
(EM, 252-253)

DEMOCRACY A HYPOTHESIS NOT A DOGMA

One of Maslow's deep concerns was with democracy. To him the
healthy person was a democratic person. We have seen above that
the self-actualizing person has a democratic personality. And we have
seen the importance of democracy in the work situation.

However, theories of democracy and liberalism should not be
accepted as pieties and dogmas, instead they should be treated as
research questions, to be verified (or not) scientifically. It is not that
Maslow disapproved of democracy and liberalism, but that as a scientist he believed that everything ought to be verified.

> [P]olitical democracy is an experiment which is based upon
> a scientifically unproven assumption: namely that human
> beings like to participate in their own fate, that given suffi-
> cient information they will make wise decisions about their
> own lives, and that they prefer freedom to being bossed, that
> they prefer to have a say in everything which affects their
> future, etc. None of these assumptions have been adequately
> enough proven so that we would call it scientific fact in about
> the same way that we would label biological fact scientific.
> We have to know more about these psychological factors
> than we do. Because this is so, we ought to again be very
> aware, very conscious, of the fact that these are articles of
> faith rather than articles of final knowledge... (EM, 54-55)

DIFFERENCES IN BIOLOGICAL GIFTS

One of the dogmas in democratic theory is that everybody is equal. When it comes to biological gifts, this is not so. "If all newborn infants were given complete equality of opportunity, all sorts of individual differences in capacity, talent, intelligence, strength, etc., would appear during the life span. What to do about these?" (FR, 219)

As social justice improves, our awareness of these biological differences will sharpen. "The more we continue to reduce social injustice, the more we shall find this replaced by 'biological injustice,' by the fact that babies are born into the world with different genetic potentials." (M&P, xviii-xvix)

At one extreme of biological gifts, there are many people who are not able to exercise their citizenship:

> It's a funny thing how this whole delicate problem is ducked by everybody in the whole society. For instance, we talk about every man having a vote while the fact is that a good 10 or 20 percent of the population don't have votes and never will. For instance, the people who are locked up in jails and insane asylums, who are feeble-minded, who are physically so handicapped that they live in hospitals all their lives and can't move, the senile people who have to be taken care of, the helpless cripples, and god knows how many other kinds of people. (EM, 135)

At the other end of biological gifts, we find individuals who are superior at everything:

None of the writers that I have been reading on management dares to confront the profound political implications of the fact which is so unpopular in any democracy that some people are superior to others in any given skill or capacity and also that there is some evidence to indicate that some people tend to be generally superior, that they are simply superior biological organisms born into the world. For the latter I can use the Terman kind of data which indicates that all desirable traits tend to correlate positively…. (EM, 133)

Lewis Terman about forty years ago selected children with high IQs and then tested them in many ways through the succeeding decades and up to the present time. "His general finding was that children chosen because they were superior in intelligence were superior in everything else as well. The great generalization that he wound up with was that all desirable traits in a human being correlate positively." (FR, 6)

Democratic dogma tries to suppress these differences in biological gifts, but in fact such differences do not really hinder democracy:

What I smell here is again some of the democratic dogma and piety in which all people are equal and in which the conception of a factually stronger person or natural leader or dominant person or superior intellect or superior decisiveness or whatever is bypassed because it makes everybody uncomfortable and because it seems to contradict the democratic philosophy (of course, it does not really contradict it). (EM, 187)

HOW TO CHOOSE LEADERS

Individuals with unsatisfied basic needs often seek power in order to satisfy them. These individuals should not have power.

> [T]he person who seeks for power is the one who is just exactly likely to be the one who shouldn't have it, because he neurotically and compulsively needs power. Such people are apt to use power very badly; that is, use it for overcoming, overpowering, hurting people, ... they use it for their own selfish gratifications, conscious and unconscious, neurotic as well as healthy. The task, the job, the objective requirements of the situation tend to be ... lost in the shuffle when such a person is the leader. He is essentially looking out for himself, for a kind of self-cure of neurosis, for a self-gratification. (EM, 125)

Leaders should be chosen who are best suited to the job at hand: "Any good society that hopes to grow must be able to choose as leaders those individuals who are best suited for the job in fact, in actual talents, and capacity." (FR, 222-223)

The bottom line is that leaders should not be able to self-select: "It is clear that, in the long run, one cannot rely on self-selection for supplying leaders and therapists." (EM, 185)

SOCIETAL ACHIEVEMENTS DEVALUED

One consequence of basic needs gratification is that gratified needs drop out of consciousness. Something similar happens in society. As society ameliorates an injustice, that injustice drops out of consciousness, people see only the tasks ahead, and many may think little or no progress has been made.

> [T]he blessings we have already achieved come to be taken for granted, to be forgotten, to drop out of consciousness, and finally, even, not to be valued any more—at least until they are taken away from us. For instance, it is characteristic of the American culture as I write this preface in January, 1970, that the undoubted advancements and improvements that have been struggled for and achieved through 150 years are being flicked aside by many thoughtless and shallow people as being all a fake, as being of no value whatsoever, as being unworthy of fighting for or protecting, or valuing, just because the society is not yet perfect. (M&P, xvi)

XI. Religion

AT THE BEGINNING of every religion is a peak experience, which is then cloaked in whatever mythology lies at hand.

> The very beginning, the intrinsic core, the essence, the universal nucleus of every known high religion ... has been the private, lonely, personal illumination, revelation, or ecstasy of some acutely sensitive prophet or seer ... That is to say ... that these older reports ... were, in fact, perfectly natural, human peak-experiences which are then phrased in terms of whatever conceptual, cultural, and linguistic framework the particular seer has available in his time. (Religion, 35)

Peak experiences are real, but the religions founded on them are arbitrary: "[W]hatever is different about these illuminations can fairly be taken to be localisms both in time and space, and are, therefore, peripheral, expendable, not essential." (Religion, 36) "The explanations that these people offered for these achievements have nothing in common with each other and need not be considered seriously." (M&P, 244)

What starts as a peak experience often congeals into dogma, which then tends to deny further peak experiences: "Organized Religion, the churches, finally may become the major enemies of the religious experience and the religious experiencer." (Religion, 5)

In fact, there is no need for organized religion at all, because every person has their own peak experiences, therefore their own private religion.

From the point of view of the peak-experiencer, each person has his own private religion, which he develops out of his own private revelations in which are revealed to him his own private myths and symbols, rituals and ceremonials, which may be of the profoundest meaning to him personally and yet completely idiosyncratic, i.e., of no meaning to anyone else. But to say it even more simply, each "peaker" discovers, develops, and retains his own religion (Religion, 42)

The peak experience is a part of our biology. There is no need to invoke the supernatural. "Explanation from the natural is more parsimonious and therefore more satisfying to educated people than is explanation from the supernatural." (Religion, 53) "[T]he concept of supernatural beings ... doesn't seem to be of any great consequence except for the comfort of the individual himself." (Religion, 73)

God is an arbitrary choice of the individual. "Whether or not to call this integration 'God' finally gets to be an arbitrary decision and a personal indulgence..." (Religion, 74)

XII. Science

MASLOW WAS DEEPLY concerned with the science of psychology, and sought to reform it. In this regard he continually touted Michael Polanyi's *Personal Knowledge: Towards a Post-Critical Philosophy* as a key inspiration.

ORTHODOX SCIENCE

DOES NOT WORK FOR HUMAN BEINGS

Psychology is a science, but the methods of classical science do not work well for the study of human beings.

The method for all the sciences was based on that of physics and astronomy: "It was primarily the physicists and the astronomers who created ... the subculture known as Science (including all its goals, methods, axiomatic values, concepts, languages, folkways, prejudices, selective blindnesses, hidden assumptions)." (Science, 5)

These methods were developed in order to investigate impersonal phenomena. Here the ethic of investigation was to be emotionally uninvolved with what was studied.

> Classically, 'scientific objectivity' has been most successfully achieved when its objects were most distant from human aspirations, hopes, and wishes. It is easy to feel uninvolved, detached, clear-eyed, and neutral if one is studying the nature of rocks or heat or electrical currents. (Science, 64)

The human being was never a suitable object of study under this scientific methodology. To apply scientific methods to human beings is "simply a more difficult, more exasperating application of the methodology of physics, astronomy, biology, etc., to an irritatingly unsuitable object. ... The human being is "a special case ... a peripheral example on the edge of impersonal scientific method." (Science, 57)

In fact, "Orthodox science has been a failure in all the human and social realms..." (Science, 79)

"For knowing human beings the usual procedures of physical science are practically useless." (Science, 12)

VALUE-FREE SCIENCE

Orthodox science also desperately wanted to be value-free, but values are at the heart of human nature.
Nineteenth-century science:

> mistakenly conceived of itself as having nothing to say about ends or ultimate values or spiritual values. This is the same as saying that these ends are entirely outside the range of natural human knowledge, that they can never be known in a confirmable, validated way... (Religion, 28)

Such a value-free science abdicates much of experience. Orthodox science has excluded many cognitive problems "because of its hidden but fatal weakness — its inability to deal impersonally with the personal, with the problems of value, of individuality, of consciousness, of beauty, of transcendence, of ethics." (Science, 5)

In particular, a value-free science banishes "from the realm of the respectably knowable" all experiences of transcendence, "awe, wonder, mystery, ecstasy, beauty, and peak experiences." (Science, 67)

Emotions were banished alongside values:

> Orthodox science today attempts to be free not only of values but also of emotions ... The basic notions of detachment and objectivity, of precision, rigor, and quantification, of parsimony, and of lawfulness, all imply that emotion and emotional intensity are contaminants of cognition. (Science, 66)

AMORAL SCIENCE

A science that is value-free is also amoral:

> Such an attitude dooms science to be nothing more than technology, amoral and nonethical (as the Nazi doctors taught us). Such a science can be no more than a collection of instrumentalities, methods, techniques, nothing but a tool to be used by any man, good or evil, and for any ends, good or evil. (Religion, 28-29)

Such a science is "even anti-human, merely technology which can be bought by anyone for any purpose, like the German 'scientists' who could work with equal zeal for Nazis, for Communists, or for Americans." (Religion, 32)

METHODS FOR KNOWING HUMAN BEINGS

There are, however, methods for knowing human beings that work better than those of orthodox science.

CLINICAL KNOWLEDGE

To begin with, to know human beings, it is best to turn to the clinic: "Most of what we know of human motivation comes not from psychologists but from psychotherapists treating patients." (M&P, 33) "We may then regard these techniques of therapy and self-discovery as being also cognitive tools or scientific methods." (Science, 68) "More valuable than orthodox science in the study of human beings is clinical knowledge, that is, knowledge gleaned from working with human beings in analysis or therapy." (Science, 68)

> [I]nsofar as I was a psychotherapist, an analysand, a father, a teacher, and a student of personality — that is, insofar as I dealt with whole persons — "scientific psychology" gradually proved itself to be of little use. In this realm of persons I found far greater sustenance in "psychodynamics", especially the psychologies of Freud and Adler, psychologies that were clearly not "scientific" by the definitions of the day. (*Science*, 11)

HOW TO KNOW INDIVIDUALS

Physical science works with classes of objects, not individuals. "There are no individuals in a textbook of physics or chemistry, let alone mathematics." (Science, 12)

In psychology, however, each person must be approached "as an individual unique and peculiar, the sole member of his class." (Science, 12)

If we want to know human beings, we must interact with them:

> By far the best way we have to learn what people are like is to get them, one way or another, to tell us… This can be done directly, or indirectly by free association, paintings, dreams, stories, gestures, which are then interpreted. (Science, 13)

However, this method of inquiry poses problems of its own:

The person can lie. "For example, a person who is telling us his political attitude is, so to speak, the only witness to what he is reporting. He can easily fool us if he wants to." (Science, 13)

The person has to permit themself to be known. "He must accept and trust the knower, and even get to love him…" (Science, 16)

The person's purposes may be unconscious. "Our problems are further complicated by the fact that his purposes can be unknown to the person himself." (Science, 16).

"Any comprehensive psychology of science will have to go into great detail about the relations of consciousness to the unconscious and to the preconscious, and of so-called 'primary process' cognition to 'secondary process' cognition." (Science, 16-17)

Taoistic receptivity in therapy is a key technique for learning about individuals. Taoistic knowing is nonintrusive and receptive, allowing the knowledge to appear rather than actively pursuing it.

"That is, the thing to do is to do nothing." (Science, 55)

> It may be a little inexact to call Taoistic receptivity a technique, for it consists essentially in being able to keep your hands off and your mouth shut, to be patient, to suspend action and be receptive and passive. It stresses careful observation of a noninterfering sort. (Science, 53)
>
> The best known operation of this kind is Freud's discovery of (and recommendation of) free-floating attention. In trying to understand a therapeutic patient — or, for that matter, any person — it turns out to be most efficient in the long run to give up active concentration and striving to understand quickly. (Science, 54)

"The psychoanalyst's injunction is, 'Let the unconscious speak to (and listen to) the unconscious.'" (Science, 54)

KNOWING THROUGH FUSION

We have seen above in *Qualities of Self-actualizating Persons* that love, especially self-actualizing love, improves perception. The farthest reach of love is fusion. "The endpoint of knowing through love is fusion with the object of love, that is, becoming one with it ..." (Science, 62)

ABRAHAM H. MASLOW

The ultimate limit, the completion toward which this kind of interpersonal knowledge moves, is through intimacy to the mystical fusion in which the two people become one in a phenomenological way that has been best described by mystics, Zen Buddhists, peak experiencers, lovers, estheticians, etc. In this experience of fusion a knowing of the other comes about through becoming the other, i.e., it becomes experiential knowledge from within. I know it because I know myself, and It has now become part of myself. (Science, 57)

"If you become the other, then you can answer many questions about them simply by introspection." (Science, 62-63)

HEALTHY AND UNHEALTHY KNOWERS

Poor psychological health results in poor knowing. "Scientists who are deficiency-motivated and safety-need-motivated are ego-centered. Their pursuit of knowing is used to gratify their personal emotional difficulties." (Science, 19)

Conversely, improved psychological health improves knowing. "Once we get our personal problems solved, then we can get truly interested in the world for its own sake." (Science, 19) "The injunction might read, then: make yourself into a good instrument of knowledge. Cleanse yourself as you would the lenses of your microscope." (Science, 30)

The healthy scientist is a more creative scientist. "Richard Craig has demonstrated an almost complete overlap between the personality characteristics of creative men listed by Torrance and those that I had listed for self-actualizing people. The two concepts in fact seem almost to be the same." (Science, 26)

We have seen above that self-actualizers have more efficient perception of reality because their needs are gratified.

> [S]elf-actualizing people distinguished far more easily than most the fresh, the concrete, and the idiographic from the generic, abstract, and rubricized. The consequence is that they live more in the real world of nature than in the man-made mass of concepts, abstractions, expectations, beliefs, and stereotypes that most people confuse with the world. (M&P, 154)

This superior perception further results in "a superior ability to reason, to perceive the truth, to come to conclusions, to be logical and to be cognitively efficient, in general." (M&P, 154)

Peak experiences, too, are methods of knowing:

> [E]sthetic joys may also be cognitive signs, like signal rockets that go off to tell us we have found something important. It is in the peak experiences that Being-cognition is most likely to take place. In such moments we are perhaps most able to see into the heart of things. (Science, 75).

FROM EXPERIENCE TO SCIENCE

SCIENCE STARTS WITH EXPERIENCE

"[A]ll of life must first be known experientially. There is no substitute for experience, none at all." (Science, 29)

"[T]he first task of the scientist is to experience truly that which exists." (Science, 45)

ABRAHAM H. MASLOW

CHAOTIC AND INEFFABLE EXPERIENCE

Though experience may be chaotic and almost ineffable, it nonethe-
less can be the raw material of science. "Confronted with the depths
of human nature, we psychologists learn to respect also the inarticu-
late, the preverbal and subverbal, the tacit, the ineffable, the mythic,
the archaic, the symbolic, the poetic, the esthetic." (Science, 16-17)

> The inexact, the illogical, the metaphorical, the mythic, the
> symbolic, the contradictory or conflicted, the ambiguous,
> the ambivalent... It is not yet understood that they are char-
> acteristic of the human being at his highest levels of devel-
> opment as well as at his lowest, and that they can be valued,
> used, loved, built upon, rather than just being swept under
> the rug. (Religion, 58)

Knowledge during the initial stages of scientific investigation is also
chaotic:

In the first stage of knowledge "... all that we have to deal with are
hunches, guesses, intuitions, dreams, fantasies, vague 'pre-thoughts'
not yet verbalized." (Science, 71)

"In a word, the rules, principles or laws of the explorer or the
scout are different from the rules suitable for later settlers simply
because the tasks are different." (Science, 74)

HUMANITIES ARE A SOURCE OF EXPERIENCE

"Science is only one means of access to knowledge of natural, social,
and psychological reality. The creative artist, the philosopher, the

82

literary humanist, or for that matter, the ditch digger, can also be the discoverer of truth..." (M&P, 8)

"I see no way of sharply defining off scientists from nonscientists." (M&P, 9)

> If we define science as a search for truth, insight, and understanding, and as a concern with important questions, we must be hard put to it to differentiate between the scientist on the one hand, and the poets, artist, and philosophers on the other hand. (M&P, 14)

EXPERIENCE, HOWEVER, MUST BE VERIFIED

It is essential to verify experience: "Poets, prophets, priests, dramatists, artists, and diplomats may have wonderful insights, but it is possible for the great insight (peak experience) to be mistaken..." (Being, 89)

Psychologists are only too aware of the shortcomings and even impossibility of a pure and sole introspectionism. We know too much of hallucinations, delusions, illusions, denials, repressions, and other defenses against knowing reality." (Science, 29-30)

"If you go into the desert and discover some unexpected mine or some improbable animal, your experiential knowledge may be certain and valid, but you can hardly expect others to believe you entirely and on faith. They also have a right to see for themselves..." (Science, 40)

Individual experience "cannot be a substitute for the routine skeptical and cautious procedures of science." (Being, 89)

SCIENCE THEN CODIFIES EXPERIENCE

"My thesis is that experiential knowledge is prior to verbal-conceptual knowledge but that they are hierarchically-integrated and need each other." (Science, 29)

"First comes 'knowing' in the experiential sense; then come the checks on the fallibilities of the senses and of experiential knowledge; then come the abstractions, the theories, i.e., orthodox science." (Science, 29-30)

> [S]cience has two tasks. One is the full acknowledgment, acceptance, and savoring of concrete, raw experience. The other is the effort to bind these experiences together, to seek out their similarities and differences, to figure out their regularities and their interrelations with each other, to construct them into systems... (Science, 49)

THE OBLIGATION OF SCIENCE
TO INCLUDE ALL OF REALITY

Science must include all that exists.

> If there is any primary rule of science, it is, in my opinion, acceptance of the obligation to acknowledge and describe all of reality, all that exists, everything that is the case. Before all else science must be comprehensive and all-inclusive. It must accept within its jurisdiction even that which it cannot understand or explain, that for which no theory exists, that which cannot be measured, predicted, controlled, or ordered.

It must accept even contradictions and illogicalities and mysteries, the vague, the ambiguous, the archaic, the unconscious, and all other aspects of existence that are difficult to communicate. At its best it is completely open and excludes nothing. It has no "entrance requirements". Furthermore it includes all levels or stages of knowledge, including the inchoate. Knowledge has an embryology, too; it cannot confine itself to its final and adult forms alone. Knowledge of low reliability is also part of knowledge. (Science, 42)

In principle, at least, science should be capable of generating normative psychologies of psychotherapy, of personal development, of eupsychian or utopian social psychology, of religion, of work, play, and leisure, of esthetics, of economics, and politics, and who knows what else? (Science, 5)

"It is, so to speak, an open-door policy... Any question can be asked, any problem raised." (Science, 34)

"The only requirement is to do the best you can with the problem at the time and under the circumstances." (Science, 34)

Even religion can be studied scientifically. "Once science is broadened and redefined, the basic religious questions can be accepted as a proper part of the jurisdiction of science." (Religion, 28)

[I]t is increasingly clear that the religious questions ... are perfectly respectable scientifically, that they are rooted deep in human nature, that they can be studied, described, examined in a scientific way, and that the churches were trying to answer perfectly sound human questions. (Religion, 34-35)

A SCIENCE OF LOVE AND VALUE

SCIENCE IN PURSUIT OF VALUE

Far from being value-free, even orthodox science is in pursuit of value. "[T]he whole enterprise of science is concerned with 'Truth' ... And of course, truth has always been counted among the ultimate values. That is to say, science is in the service of a value, and so are all scientists." (Science, 68)

Science can provide scientists with B-values and peak experiences. "Science at its highest level is ultimately the organization of, the systematic pursuit of, and the enjoyment of wonder, awe, and mystery. The greatest rewards that the scientist can have are such peak-experiences and B-cognitions as these." (Science, 82)

> The process of acquiring knowledge ... and the contemplation and enjoyment of it is turning out to be one of the richest sources of esthetic raptures, of semireligious ecstasies, of experiences of awe and mystery. Such emotional experiences are among the ultimate joys of living. (Science, 75).

Science can be the "poetry of the intellect." (Science, 81)

A SCIENTIFIC ETHIC OF LOVE

Ultimately, for all the sciences, we might better replace the ethic of objectivity with an ethic of love. Love improves perception, and the loving scientist does better work.

The good scientist is a loving scientist. "[W]e might formulate a general hypothesis to read so: love for the object seems likely to enhance experiential knowledge of the object, with lack of love diminishing experiential knowledge of the object…" (Science, 31)

> Researcher A is really fascinated with schizophrenics (or white rats or lichens). Researcher B, however, is much more interested in manic-depressive insanity (or monkeys or mushrooms). We may confidently expect that Researcher A will (a) freely choose or prefer to study schizophrenics, etc., (b) work better and longer at it, be more patient, more stubborn, more tolerant of associated chores, (c) have more hunches, intuitions, dreams, illumination about them, (d) be more likely to make more profound discoveries about schizophrenia, and (e) the schizophrenics will feel easier with him and say that he "understands" them. In all these respects he would almost certainly do better than Researcher B. (Science, 31-32)

"The truth is that the really good scientist often does approach his work with love, devotion, and self-abnegation, as if he were entering into a holy of holies." (Science, 78)

"Therefore, can we consider changing the paradigm of scientific exploration from objective knowing to knowing through love?" (Science, 60)

A Personal Critique

Maslow's theory of human nature is based on the clinical findings of himself and many other psychologists, psychoanalysts, psychotherapists, anthropologists, and the like. His motivation theory "was an effort to integrate into a single theoretical structure the partial truths I saw in Freud, Adler, Jung, D. M. Levy, Fromm, Horney, and Goldstein." (M&P, xi) At other times Maslow listed many others whose work he had learned from: James, Dewey, Wertheimer, Reich, Rogers, Bühler, May, Grof, Dabrowski, Murray, Sutich, Bugental, Allport, Frankl, Murphy, Rorschach, "and many, many others". (M&P, 35, 271) Maslow's Journals show his mind at work absorbing the writings and research of these others.

As well, Maslow found corroboration for the particular concept of self-actualization in the work of many thinkers. "Among psychiatrists, psychoanalysts, and psychologists it has been found necessary by Goldstein, Bühler, Jung, Horney, Fromm, Rogers, and many others." (M&P, 78) Maslow also "tapped the immense literatures of mysticism, religion, art, creativeness, love, etc." (Being, 66)

Yet Maslow himself tells us that his theory, however useful in the clinic, has not been verified in the laboratory.

> It is fair to say that this theory has been quite successful in a clinical, social and personological way, but not in a laboratory and experimental way. It has fitted very well with the personal experience of most people, and has often given them a structured theory that has helped them to make

better sense of their inner lives. It seems for most people to have a direct, personal, subjective plausibility. *And yet it still lacks experimental verification and support.* I have not yet been able to think of a good way to put it to the test in the laboratory. (M&P, xii, emphasis added)

Maslow also admitted that he had not taken the time to set up laboratory experiments.

It's just that I haven't got the time to do careful experiments myself … They take too long, in view of the years that I have left and the extent of what I want to do. So I myself do only 'quick-and-dirty' little pilot explorations, mostly with a few subjects only, inadequate to publish but enough to convince myself that they are probably true and will be confirmed one day. Quick little commando raids, guerrilla attacks." (Maslow, quoted in Grogan, *Encountering America*, location 1987)

Maslow also pointedly admitted that his work on self-actualization had flaws. He did so because he was concerned that people would go haring off taking his theories as gospel, which many indeed did.

The same thing is true of my studies of self-actualizing people— there is only this one study of mine available. There were many things wrong with the sampling, so many in fact that it must be considered to be, in the classical sense anyway, a bad or poor or inadequate experiment. I am quite willing to concede this—as a matter of fact, I am eager to concede it—because I'm a little worried about this stuff which I consider to be tentative being swallowed whole by all sorts of enthusiastic people… (EM, 55-56)

Again, addressing management theorist Douglas McGregor's claims about the positive effects of good management in the workplace, Maslow commented that the evidence is "practically nil". (EM, 56)

> ... [A] good deal of the evidence upon which he bases his conclusions comes from my researches and my papers on motivations, self-actualization, actualization, etc. But I of all people should know just how shaky this is as a final foundation. My work on motivations came from the clinic, from a study of neurotic people. (EM, 55)

Perhaps Maslow was too harsh on himself. He was all too interested in making his work conform ultimately to the precepts of orthodox science. But he had long ago abandoned orthodox science as inapplicable to human beings. It would not be surprising therefore if orthodox scientific proof is not to be had.

One "proof" of his theories is that they have "gone to the people". His concepts of *the hierarchy of needs, self-actualization, peak experiences, and transcendence* have infiltrated much of our psychological and business cultures.

There are books that purport to update Maslow's work, to show where it is proven and unproven, based on experiment. In particular, see Scott Kaufman's *Transcend: The New Science of Self-actualization*.

SCIENCE STOPS AT THE SUPERNATURAL

Maslow insisted that science include all that exists. For him this meant science ought expand to include all human experience, however chaotic and ineffable.

But, in fact, Maslow does not include all experience. He draws a line. Peak experiencers are not allowed to have access to the supernatural. They may think they have such access. But, according to Maslow, it is really their biology that is speaking. In his words: "Explanation from the natural is more parsimonious and therefore more satisfying to educated people than is explanation from the supernatural." (Religion, 53)

This is clearly drawing a line based not on experience but on principle. The principle is humanism, that there is nothing superhuman, we have only our biology.

Maslow argues elsewhere that the lover sees the beloved more clearly, the SA lover sees most clearly, and the SA scientist in love investigates more clearly. We may argue similarly that the peak experiencer, in love at the moment, sees more clearly. Perhaps when they think they see God, they really have seen Him.

The question arises, where do peak experiences come from? These experiences so vital and regenerative, where in our "biology" do they come from? From our genes? From our brains? Probably the best way to find this out would be to follow Maslow's method: Ask the human being who has them. But Maslow thinks whatever human beings say about their peak experiences are "localisms", they are "peripheral, expendable, not essential". (Religion, 36) "The explanations ... have nothing in common ... and need not be considered seriously." (M&P, 244)

The content of peak experiences we may call revelation. There are problems with revelation for the scientist. We all have peak experiences; but the content of peak experiences depends on our disparate imaginations; our imaginations differ wildly. How is science to verify, analyze, and codify the content of these experiences? How to determine what is true, and what is not true? So Maslow draws a line: peak experiences reveal our humanity, but they do not reveal the supernatural, whatever the experiencer may think.

<h2 style="text-align:center">HOW TO?</h2>

Maslow describes several ways to grow psychologically. It is clear from history and the state of the world that for the mass of humanity these have not worked. Maslow says so himself.

"Though, in principle, self-actualization is easy, in practice it rarely happens (by my criteria, certainly in less than 1% of the adult population)." (Being, 190)

Even the interventions Maslow suggests do not work for most.

"[S]ince therapy is impracticable for mass purposes, most people simply stay caught in the situation and lead privately and publicly miserable lives." (Religion, 54)

As for the changes Maslow suggests in education and the workplace, these have not been adopted in any widespread manner, and it is not clear what agency would set them in motion. Further, it is not clear who or what would start the slow revolution he calls for.

To become the *good person* therefore remains an individual choice. And the *good society* remains a utopian ideal.

In the end, Maslow throws up his arms somewhat in jest, "What does one do when he self-actualizes? Does he grit his teeth and squeeze?" (FR, 45)

Selected Further Reading

Papers and Journals of Maslow:

The following were consulted but not included in this synopsis:

Dominance, Self-Esteem, Self-Actualization: Germinal Papers of A.H. Maslow; ed. Richard J. Lowry, 1993.

Future Visions: The Unpublished Papers of Abraham Maslow, ed. Edward Hoffman, 1996.

Politics and Innocence: A Humanistic Debate, May, Rogers, Maslow, et. al., 1986.

New Knowledge in Human Values, ed. Abraham H. Maslow, 1959.

The Journals of A.H. Maslow, ed. Richard J. Lowry, 1979.

There are also a number of uncollected papers.

A full Maslow bibliography is available online.

Scholarly Biographies of Maslow:

A.H. Maslow: An Intellectual Portrait, Richard J. Lowry, 1973.

The Right to be Human: A Biography of Abraham Maslow, Edward Hoffman, rev. 1999.

Histories of Humanistic Psychology:

Encountering America: Humanistic Psychology, Sixties Culture and the Shaping of the Modern Self, Jessica Grogan, 2013.

Social Amnesia: A Critique of Contemporary Psychology, Russell Jacoby, 1997.

Journeys of Faith: Religion, Spirituality, & Humanistic Psychology, Mike Brock, 2020.

An Update to Maslow:

Transcend: The New Science of Self-Actualization, Scott Barry
  Kaufman, 2020.

CITATIONS

Citations are for the kindle versions except *The Farther Reaches of
Human Nature* and *Eupsychian Management,* for which no kindle ver-
sion is available.

www.ingramcontent.com/pod-product-compliance
Lightning Source LLC
Chambersburg PA
CBHW052118030426
42335CB00025B/3044